The Referral Marketing System...
A Step-By-Step Guide To Turning Your Business Into A Referral Generating Machine

What Others Are Saying About The Referral Marketing System Step By Step Guide:

"Michael hasn't just written a book he has compiled a comprehensive blueprint for success and included the tools to implement it. I have personally built multiple 6 and 7 figure businesses using the same philosophy as Michael. It's all about the relationships. Unfortunately while reading this book I have found so many ways I could have done things better and found myself wishing this book was around many years ago. Whether you are an experienced business person or just starting out, this book and the resources in it will fast track growth in a most cost effective way. Even now I will be going back to a few chapters and implementing some great strategies." - **Steve Brossman, The Authority Catalyst, www.stevebrosman.com**

"This book is a no-nonsense guide to filling your business up with referrals. Michael is the "go-to" expert in this field. We use his strategies successfully in our business" - **Robert Coorey, MBA, Best-Selling Author,** *Feed A Starving Crowd*

"This is why Michael Griffiths is the number one authority on Referral marketing… This easy to use, practical, step by step approach on growing your business through referral marketing is a MUST READ! Michael has clearly articulated the Why, What and How you go about fast tracking your business through the power of referral marketing." – **James Short, Founder,** Goals Tribe

1

Whether you're a start up, or a seasoned business owner, you need to get your hands on The Referral Marketing System. I've always understood the power of nurturing and building solid relationships to help grow y businesses, but have had so much trial and error over the years.

Michael has broken down his referral marketing system into easily actionable steps, and he clearly outlines the strategy for building a successful referral network. Some of his ideas are so simple, I was scratching my head thinking "Why didn't I think of that?"

Through Michael's case studies, I was able to clearly see opportunities I'd previously left on the table which I'll now be implementing to achieve even greater success. – **Samantha Riley, CEO and Founder Of The Accelerant Group**

This book is a practical guide on what to do to build your own powerful referral network. Michael Griffiths explains in detail the rationale for his strategies as well as what you need to do to get the best results. The action steps at the end of each chapter help immensely with taking these ideas from "oh yeah... I should do that" to be part of your daily routine. Highly recommended! – **Esther Kiss Founder of** **"Born To Influence"**

Foreword:

I'm writing this book to share principles that are commonly known but rarely have such detail or process built around them, which is what is needed to be a success.

Having created 7 businesses, all of them through referrals, cross promotions, affiliates and strategic partnerships, I have been able to create the right systems and processes to grow any business in the same way. This is what I will share with you in the hope you can do exactly the same thing.

This book is not about theory, it is about action and doing the things that are outlined in every chapter. It is about having a go and getting rid of all self-doubt and just doing it (as Nike would say).

Referral Marketing is not new. However, only a handful of people take it to the extent that I do in this book. Many marketing people tell you that referral marketing works, but them themselves don't understand the step-by-step process that is required to have a funnel full of new business opportunities. They just understand that it needs to be done and rely on luck for it to happen – there's rarely an explanation of "how" to become a master referral marketer.

"Luck" really doesn't have much of anything to do with success. You have the same opportunities that internationally listed companies have in creating partnerships. Those that get out and ask the right questions will be those that get the great opportunities. I encourage you to be that person.

Like with everything in business and life, the more we can turn it into a system with goals and steps, the easier it is to do. There are plenty of tools that allow you to automate the process, to keep it organised and to save you time and effort. So I encourage you to use those as often as you can.

Every business should have referral partners, cross promotion partners and affiliates. This means that you have other people filling your sales funnel for you. This is true leverage. It is this leverage that will see your business grow quicker than ever before.

And finally thank you to all those in our community which have provide me with the opportunity to always get better, create better systems and process for others to follow. I look forward to connecting with you and hearing more about yourself and your business!

Michael

Table of Contents

Introduction:

Business is a funny world! Products, services, technology, distribution, people all put into a big pot and in the end some people win and others lose.

We have seen a lot over the past 20 years. The internet craze that bought us all closer together, the smarter computers and phones that keep us connected and the social media world allows you to find out what people are doing at anytime you want.

We are used to being "connected" and have information at our fingertips 24/7, and yet, there is one key element of business that has remained unchanged… one thing in common that has been tried and tested over time.

For the master connectors, this element has doubled, tripled and quadrupled their business at a minimum cost.

That key element is "Relationships."

Relationship marketing, as some call it, never fades in and out as other fads. One day there is Facebook and Linkedin and the next day a new, shiny app comes out that becomes the new "must-join." Whatever these means are in the digital age, people always have the need to meet others and to have the human element of connection.

Those business owners who work on having a referral marketing system, work on building relationships each day and work on staying front of mind, will always have new business, repeat business and an endless supply of prospects through referrals.

Getting business through referrals or word of mouth doesn't just happen. There is an art and skill, a process, a system and a way that ensures you get new opportunities daily rather than just here and there.

Referral marketing is by far the cheapest way to grow a business. You can spend $500, $1,000 or $5,000+ on Google ads before you get any traction, $500+ per month on SEO and still you probably won't hit the front page, $1,000's on direct mail, social media campaigns, flyers, etc and yet you will probably not see even a 1% return.

Marketing has changed and those that change today with it will ensure their business growth. Let's explore the new world of referral marketing 'done right.'

In each chapter we will look at the typical businessperson, the problems that are created and then the solution for a successful referral plan.

This book has been written from years of experience, it is the step-by-step process to getting as many referrals and new opportunities each day as you need. We have seen people get 1 or 2 and others get 6 or 7. How many you get is all up to how many you need!

This book is very action orientated, setting out at the end of each chapter exactly what you need to do and how I can help you immediately as well. It should only take 45 minutes to read but the value and steps it shows you will be invaluable for life.

Chapter 1: Your Mind Is The Gateway To The Gold

I'm sure you have probably heard the way you think determines your outcomes and no, this is not a personal development book… however, you can only be a success in generating referrals if you think the right way, act the right way and have the right intentions.

We are bought up in a very competitive world. We start school at 5 and straight away we are measured against other children, who can write better, spell better and who have the better maths skills, sporting skills, music skills. As we get older that gets more intense with private schools, selective schools and scholarship offerings. We are taught to win, to go all out for ourselves, to beat others, to be selfish.

The problem is: in the business world, those people generally lose.

Business success is about collaboration, building partnerships and for helping one another to be successful. For that to happen, people have to think a certain way: in terms of relationships, not cutthroat competition.

Every day we have millions of thoughts, ideas and processes that go through our head… some great, others good and many not at all helpful to us. Our brain is filtering what we listen to, what we act on and how we act on it.

A business owner often has their own survival front of mind, so they focus on activities that help themselves and often forget the power of other people and helping others.

Here is a glimpse into what it takes to develop the mindset of a successful businessperson who understands that without relationships, success comes with great difficulty – if at all.

The Successful Referral Master Has the Right Mindset

Your mind is the gateway to your success in attracting referrals into your business. There are a few things that you need to get right with yourself before you can expect others to want to help you.

1. Have an abundance mindset

Too many people go through life with a scarcity mindset, worrying that everyone else is getting more, that by giving up work someone else will get it, worrying about limited resources and a "if one person wins, the rest must lose" mentality. This mindset is characterised by taking on everything and anything that keeps their mind and business small: underselling themselves ("just to get a foot in the door"); keeping clients that are more trouble than they're worth; and losing sight of their passion and vision (their "why") in favour of fearful thinking about daily expenses.

What does the successful businessperson do differently? They think big, and they think in terms of abundance – never scarcity.

Not only do you want to think big, you want to act as if you already have plenty. I'm not suggesting spending beyond your means, but you must talk as though your are wildly successful; present a successful appearance; and always focusing on what you can do for your customers rather than what your clients can do for you (never, ever think of a customer as a dollar sign!).

Those that can act this way are ready and able to help others and in turn are ready to be helped. This person is able to give up on business that doesn't really suit them; they're able to find opportunities for others without feeling like they are missing out themselves. They become selfless rather than selfish.

2. Open your mind

There are opportunities for yourself and others all around you when you have an open mind. Unfortunately if you are scarcity-orientated, you cannot be opportunity-orientated and therefore opportunities are literally not on your radar: your brain filters them out in favour of survival-based activities. In the meantime, life and opportunities go past day after day after day. Anyone can walk around with blinkers on not seeing the outside world, or you can stop and look around you for opportunities for other people just as much as you are for yourself.

3. Ask the right questions

Quite often your results come down to the quality of questions you are asking yourself and others. Questions such as "how can I help you?", "how can I do that better?", "what do I need to do today to be successful?", "how can I overcome that challenge?" or "do you have a challenge that I can help you with?" These questions are service-orientated for the most part; they are also very mindful of the valuable lessons learned in adversity and struggle; and, they show that you are taking ownership of your decisions and behaviours and willing to learn from your mistakes!

These questions are in stark contrast to survival/scarcity/stuck in the moment questions like, "Will this sale cover this week's expenses?" "How am I going to get myself noticed?" or "If I am not awarded that project, I'm not sure we'll survive the month!"

Quality questions allow you to stand out from everyone who is asking 'stuck in the moment' questions.

Don't... It's common to ask for referrals without thinking of helping the person giving the referral. This never works. Never ask for things without being willing to do something in return.

Do what I do… Over the years I have developed a "how can I help you" mindset. When I speak to people on the phone, when I go to events or when I have meetings with others, I always like to ask at the end "How Can I Help You?"

This ensures that if they are having a problem at the moment maybe someone in my network could assist them. This then brings in referrals to other people in my network as well as being able to actually help the person whom I'm with.

When you take the focus of you and onto the other person they start to realise how much you care and when I person knows that you do care about them they are more likely to want to help you also. I know if I help enough other people achieve their goals, mine will be taken care of also.

Learn to put the other person first. Focus on how you can help them build their business, and prepare to be surprised with how eagerly they will help you in return!

Actions Steps To Take

1. Start working on your mindset. Read or listen to personal development items each day for 10 minutes – this investment in yourself will yield a huge return!
2. Write a list of questions that you can turn to that are powerful to use
3. Create some affirmations that will turn your mind into an abundance machine

How I Can Help You Immediately

It is important to be around the right sorts of people who have the right values, mindsets and values. Therefore the first thing to do is to join our communities and be around people who inspire and uplift you.

Referral Marketing Facebook Page –
www.facebook.com/referralmarketingguru

LinkedIn Referral Marketing Alumni Group (you can search for it on LinkedIn or use this link) - https://www.linkedin.com/grp/home?gid=5180030

Connect with Michael Personally on Twitter - https://twitter.com/mcjsbusiness

Chapter 2: You Can't Get Referrals With Out Referral Partners

Referrals don't fall from trees (even though that would be a nice tree to have). Referrals come from other people and to get them, you need to have trusted referral partners that know what you do and want to help you grow your business.

Too many people go to networking events, have meetings with other people and do all this activity for very little return and that's because being true referral partners is never even spoken about.

We have a choice... Meet with people, build relationships with them and hope that they will pass us a referral…

Or we can meet with people, build relationships with them and strategically plan how to pass each other referrals.

Which do you think is better?

The right referral partners can be hard to find and you might have to talk to a dozen people or more before you find that someone that meets your criteria (more on that later).

What Is A Referral Partner?

A referral partner is someone that is looking out for or creating new opportunities each day for *you* to get new business. *A referral partner wants to help you because you want to help them.* A true referral partner does not need to get commissions for passing you business as this often leads to a selfish motive instead of a real referral relationship.

How Do You Choose A Referral Partner?

Having your own criteria when picking your referral partners is extremely important. As I mentioned not everyone can be or will be your referral partner so you need to understand what sort of person you are looking for. Here are some things to think about:

- Does this person have the same sort of clients or networks as what you are looking for?
- Does this person have the time to be a referral partner?
- Does this person have the credibility with their network to be able to help you?
- Does this person want to help your business grow?
- Does this person have the right mindset and values to be able to help you?

The Successful Referral Master Casts a Wide Net

I am always looking to build new referral partners with a wide range of people who have 5 or 6 referral partners across a range of different industries. New referral partners mean new opportunities and new opportunities mean more business.

The successful referral master has conversations each day with the people they meet to see what synergies are present. They are exploring ways to do business together and support each other's visions.

As a successful referral master you are constantly training your referral partners so they understand how to help you, how to find opportunities for you and how to talk about you each day.

Don't... If you think people that have little time will make good referral partners because they have the clientele you're after, think again. People who have little time to help you now will always have little time to help you in the future. Don't pick referral partners that don't have time to help you get new business.

Do what I do… Each day I speak to both old and new people in my network about the possibilities of being referral partners. I believe that 8-12 solid referral partners are the most that anyone can handle at one time, if you're doing it properly.

I train my referral partners on how I help people through the solutions that I provide and so they know what to say to the people in their network that could become a referral for me. This training is ongoing forever, not just once, like most people do.

I plan strategically with my referral partners: some daily, others weekly and some monthly to plan how we can get more referrals into each other's businesses.

Action Steps To Take

1. Look in your current network and see if there are any possible referral partners
2. If there are, contact them and speak to them about what you'd like to do
3. If you don't have any possible partners, go out to business events and find them
4. Start building your partners and training them
5. Repeat the steps until you have at least 5-6
6. Strategise with your referral partners regularly

How I Can Help You Immediately

We use a very structured way to teach our referral partners called our Referral Training Manual. It is a simple 10-page document that you give to your partners and train them on how to pass business to you.

If you would like a copy of Michael's referral training manual please pop over to www.referralmarketingguru.com.au/manual

Case Study #1: A Professional Service Business Goes From 2 Referrals A Month To 2 Referrals A Day

Here was an accountant in a capital city. Their focus was working with small and medium businesses, getting their structures right, doing tax planning, working with business owners to ensure they had cash flow and were being profitable.

There were plenty of businesses in their catchment area BUT they just were not getting any new prospects into their sales funnel.

They went to 2 or 3 networking events each month, handed out a lot of business cards, had a presence on LinkedIn but really didn't do anything to promote themselves.

They picked up 1 or 2 referrals each month from their current clients, a financial planner and a solicitor that they had had relationships with for nearly 6 years.

Within 60 days they had started to implement the following:

1) They improved their LinkedIn profile to be more personal, they got recommendations from their current clients so that other people could see how good they were and they started making posts about business accounting to show other people that they were experts in the field.

2) They created a training tool to teach their network on the sorts of referrals they wanted and then took the time to sit down with 12 key people to walk them through it.

3) They started touching base with their wider network via email and social media to stay front of mind. These were personal messages asking how the other person was.

4) They started *listening* at networking events rather than talking, they started asking lots of questions and soon realised how much value they were able to add to the other person. This then turned into the other person wanting to help them in return.

All very simple actions, but the result meant that they started to receive 1 or 2 referrals from their network every day. This was because their network understood what sort of referral they were looking for and they had strong relationships with more people than ever before.

Chapter 3: Your Network Is Your Pot Of Gold

It's great that you are looking for new referral partners and when you find them you will be a step closer to getting more referrals, but you need to also ensure that you continue to grow your network each week.

The people in your network are your pot of gold, if you use your network correctly to help them to achieve their goals. Growing your network is crucial to filling your funnel of potential new clients. So how can you do that?

Firstly we need to be aware of who is in our network and at what level. Your network includes your friends, family, business associates, people you play sports with, hang out at the bar… basically if you're around them, they're part of your network.

Sure, not everyone in your network is equal; they don't have the same influence or the same connections as each other, but everyone in your network does have networks of their own and that door can be very valuable, if you can get them to open it for you.

Your network is made up of what I call Not Known People (NK's), Known People (K's) and Active People (A's).

The 'NK' person in your network will know your name, know a bit about what you do, however they don't really have any trust with you, nor do they really understand what you do or have had any training from you on how to pass them a referral. You might get a referral from them once in a blue moon.

The 'K' person in your network will know your name, know what you do, will trust you to do a good job and they would be happy to use you themselves, however still this person has some difficulties in finding new referrals for you all the time. If the right opportunities came up when they were speaking with someone and they remembered you they would pass that referral to you. Unfortunately still it is not consistent enough.

The 'A' or active people in your network know your name, know what you do, know most things about you and the business and like you, trust you and want to help you. These people would always use you if they needed that product or service and are happy to speak to their network about you. In fact an 'A' person would even try to create an opportunity for you if you told them what you wanted them to do. These people are referral partners.

I suggest making a network list so you can take stock of who is in your network and at what level do you see them at.

The great thing with your current network is that it can change; people at a certain level can move up to become 'A' partners. It is up to you to get the right people into your network and train those who are in it to 'step it up' to help you.

The Successful Referral Master Is Always Building Their Network

The successful referral master is always adding new people into their network by attending events, meeting new people and establishing relationships.

Set yourself a goal of how many new people you would like to add to your network and then work towards it. Example: every time you attend an event concentrate on adding 6 quality people to your network.

With each new person, add them to your network database and tag them as a NK, K, or A (we will work on moving them forward in the next chapter).

The successful networker always wants to build on the relationships they have and start new ones at every chance.

Don't... If you attend events to add people to your network, don't just collect business cards and add them to your email list or connect with them on LinkedIn. You must build *relationships* with people; if you don't then they are really just a number rather than a person that is a 'K' or a 'A' in your network.

Do what I do... I have set goals around my networking and how many people I want to add to my network each month. I have goals for face-to-face networking as well as for online platforms like LinkedIn.

At each event I want to meet everyone in the room and then I want to work out who are the 6-12 people that are worth following up and building relationships with and I book those meetings for the following week.

Each person that I meet with I then decide if there is potential for a working referral relationship and if so I continue building a relationship with them and seeing how I can help them.

Action Steps To Take

1. Set a goal of how many people you want to add to your network database each week
2. Find events that will allow you to add to your network
3. Tag your new contacts as a NK, K or A
4. Build relationships with these new people

How I Can Help You Immediately

As you grow your network you are going to need a system and to be organised with your network database. Every person in your community needs to be in your system.

Here is the Database CRM System that we use personally – http://MICHAELGRIFFITHS.SENDPEPPER.COM

In here you can enter all the contact details, tag them, put them into groups and email them all at once.

Case Study #2: Saving $28,000 A Month On Advertising & Tripling Their Leads & Increasing Conversions By 35%

Here is a national business with office in every capital city of Australia, 8 in total. They were spending upwards of $52,000 a month of magazine, newspaper and TV advertising. This bought them in around 1,100 leads a month.

Their target audience were mainly female between the ages of 26-50. These people were sent to their website and landing pages to opt in for a free e-book and then an email sequence tried to get them to buy the initial service for a few hundred dollars.

Roughly 180 – 220 people would buy the product after getting the free e-book.

After looking at all their processes, we put the following in place.

1) We added a phone number field to the opt-in so that we had another way to make a touch point. This meant that after they got their e-book we could now call them to ensure that they got the book and if they had any questions.

2) We made the email sequence more conversational and got them to become part of the community on social media. This allowed us to keep in touch, add value and keep them interested for a sale down the track.

3) We started looking for other organisations that had the same target audience; places like gyms, food distributors, sporting groups, school groups, all places were females in that age group hang out.

We found roughly 200 partnerships each month were those people sent out an email for their community to come to a landing page to get the e-book as a gift from them.
This saw over 4,000 people opt in each month, a huge increase from 1,100 that they were getting.

This then allowed them to reduce their spending on their other forms of marketing.

4) This built the social media communities very quickly and allowed us to get into new networks with the number of likes, comments and shares.

5) Finally, we added two phones calls into the sequence, one 2 days after getting the e-book to check in and one 5 days after that to see how they found the e-book and talk to them about the service.

This increased the sales from 220 per month to over 350 a month and increased their button line immensely.

Just a few tweaks and finding partnership rather than paying for leads and this business had a huge turnaround in profitability.

Chapter 4: Why You Must Stay Front Of Mind Of Your People

Now that you have some referral partners, you're building your network and you're trying hard to keep relationships with them all. How do you move people from being a 'NK' to a 'K' and finally an 'A'? How do you stay front of mind so that everyone in your network remembers you and if the opportunity comes up will pass that referral to you?

Staying front of mind of your network is just as important as building your network. There is no point having them if they don't remember who you are and this will happen quickly if you aren't talking to them on a regular basis.

The idea is not to annoy them but to subtly let them know that you're around and that your focus is on helping people. How do you do that?

Today there are many ways that staying front of mind can be achieved including social media, networking events, business functions and even some out of the box ways. Here are a few of my favourites that I use each day:

Connecting - I connect people within my network each day to each other so that they can grow their network with valuable people. Instantly I'm seen as the 'go to guy' by doing so and now I have 2 people thinking of me.

Inviting - Don't ever go an event by yourself. Always ask others to come along with you. For most people going to an event is a big step and hard to do, but when they are invited by you and they get to attend with you, you are seen as the instant hero and you're remembered.

Horn Tooting - It never takes much to tell someone in your network how good someone else is. This gives that person good credibility and also the possible chance of picking up new work. If you become known as a horn tooter more and more people will want to be part of your network.

Promoting - Here is a real easy one with social media. It doesn't take much to promote something for someone else. Write and email to your network, make a post or send a message to your Facebook or LinkedIn connections o even tweet it out for them. By doing this you are not only helping them out but you are showing them that you are true to your word and follow through.

Sponsoring - Everyone today is looking for sponsors for charity events, local sporting clubs, schools, you name it everyone is raising money. Can you sponsor or donate something to the cause? What a great way to get some attention to the business, but more importantly what a great favour you have just done for that person in your network. They'll remember that one.

The Successful Referral Master Stays Front of Mind

The successful referral master makes little subtle touch points each and every day using a variety of different 'stay front of mind' techniques. They keep themselves front of mind while building stronger relationships with each of these people because they demonstrate their willingness to help others.

Each day, work on getting 5 touch points completed with your network. That might be a phone call, email, gift, letter, social media post or anything we spoke about above. Just think if you are touching 25 people in your network per week, how soon you will be being remembered and being spoken about!

Don't... every touch point you make needs to be done *for the right reason* and no, not "because Michael said to and then I'll get referrals." You need to be sincere, you need to genuinely want to help others and you need to care about how your network is doing. Therefore make the touch points for the right reason or don't do it at all!

Do what I do… At the start of each day I make a list of people who I haven't spoken to in a while from my network and put them onto my calls list. I spend 5 minutes on social media seeing whom I can help promote or invite to an event.

It doesn't take long once you are use to it and have formed a habit, but the key is you must want to build relationships with your network and *actually care about what they are doing and how you could possibly help them*.

Action Steps To Take

1. Create a list of simple touch point items that you could do for your network
2. Make a list each week of the people in your network that you want to stay front of mind with and what touch point you are going to use
3. Make notes on what you did for / with that person on your network database

How I Can Help You Immediately

We produce a "Get More Referrals" podcast every Monday. This is like having your own personal referral coach in your pocket. These podcasts are a jam packed 10 minutes of how to build new partnerships. You can get them sent to your inbox also by going to www.referralmarketingguru.com.au/podcast

Chapter 5: Be A Master Networker

It's fine staying front of mind and growing your network, but for most of us going to networking events is scary and we don't really like them. This is generally because we don't know what to 'really' do and we tend to waste a lot of time, effort and money along the way.

Networking can be fun and it is a great place to find new opportunities. You need to have the right mindset and tools before you begin your journey.

Networking is not all about you! In fact it should be 2% about you and 98% on the people you are about to meet. Why? Well you already know about yourself, but you have no idea about the other people.

Take the time at events to be a great questioner, use questions to find out more about the person you're talking to: what do they do, what challenges do they have, how could you help them, who would they like to be connected to, are they worth a follow up meeting, should they be part of your network long term.

The idea of going to networking events is to:
1. Increase your network
2. Find referral partners
3. Find referral opportunities for your network
4. Find new opportunities for yourself

Most people who attend a networking event will speak to 3 or 4 people, speak mainly about themselves and then leave with some business cards that mean nothing to them.

The Successful Referral Master Shows Interest In Others

The successful referral master is always looking for the next opportunity at a networking event. They are speaking to everyone in the room and working out who have good networks to be a part of.

They understand it is not about them pitching their own business, but finding out about the other person, as this is the only way to know if you want to do business with them. They have turned on their curiosity, and by showing of interest in the other person, they easily get them to open up and express their goals, challenges and it's a brilliant way to build rapport and trust.

Finally the successful referral masters are great follow up and follow through people. They do what they say and by when they say.

Don't... At networking events it is very easy to collect a whole bunch of business cards and then add them to your newsletter or email blasts. This is not being a referral master; this is being a pest. Those that do this have very limited success and lose credibility very quickly.

Do what I do… I go to networking events for 4 reasons and in this order:
1. To increase my network with quality people whom I know would fit well with the other people who are already in my network
2. To find new referrals for people in my current network
3. To find new referral partners where we can share each other's networks
4. To generate new business

Yes, to generate new business is last. Think about it, everyone at a networking event is 'selling'. No one wakes up and says I might go to this event tonight and I'm just going to buy.

So if you're not a seller but a connector and helper all of a sudden you stand out from the crowd.

Therefore my goal is to meet everyone in the room, find 6 people to meet with the following week and connect these new people with current people in my network.

Action Steps To Take

1. Decide what networking events best suit you and make a list for the month. Aim to attend 2-3 each month at a minimum.
2. Practice asking questions beforehand. Remember – turn on your curiosity and show genuine interest in them!
3. Have your networking tool kit ready, business cards, a name badge, pen
4. The next day follow up with people you want to connect to and start building relationships.

How I Can Help You Immediately

We run a great networking event that attracts quality people each month. If you are in Sydney, Australia you are more than welcome to come along to Monday Referral Madness. It is held on the 1st Monday of each month. (January is usually the middle of the month). Find out more at http://www.referralmarketingguru.com.au/services/sydneynetworking

Also please get our "Networking & Referral Success Kit" by going to www.referralmarketingguru.com.au and a pop up will show up for you to get your kit.

Case Study #3: No Longer Paying For Traffic, An Online Business Booms

This online business has a range of children toys. They ship all over the world and target mums and dads with children from 0 years to about 10 years of age. On average they were spending around $4,000 per month for traffic.

That got them roughly 800 unique visitors to their website each month and that created them roughly 250-350 sales. So the business was doing okay.

The marketing plan consisted on paying for ads on Facebook, on Google search and display network, banner advertising on targeted sites. Everyone wanted money to allow them to showcase their website.

That was until they found out about doing Cross Promotions!

We quickly created a list of over 1,000 other websites that had the same target audience. We made contact with each of them and suggested a simple cross promotion where they sent an email out to their customers promoting our website and we would do the same for them.

This allowed them to get in front of over 300,000 mums and dads who had children in that age range.

Within 45 days they had gone from 880 unique visitors per month to over 2,500. There sales went from 350 a month to over 1,000 sales per month and there business had become very profitable.

The best thing about all of this was they didn't have to pay for traffic anymore, so they could put that $4,000 a month back into their pockets!

The creation of cross promotions with other with the same target audience is so easy to do, but very few businesses do this. It really is as easy as:

1. Create a list of other businesses that you could promote with
2. Make contact with them and communicate your idea
3. Come up with the win/win and put an action plan in place
4. Repeat over and over again

This is great leverage of getting other people to fill your sales funnel for you.

Chapter 6: Building Your Referral Teams

You are now well on your way to becoming a referral master and having a great referral marketing system. You have referral partners, you know how to train them, you are getting a strong network and it is growing each month. You are staying front of mind of your network and creating great opportunities at the different events you are going to, and now it is time to create your own referral teams.

We have two types of teams that we want to create: a Super Group that consists of 8-10 people who will all come together each month; and a Profitability Partner who is an individual with whom you will have a strategic phone call each week.

There are plenty of referral groups out there. They all have their own ways of doing things and attract different sorts of people. Quite often only 15-20% of people in those groups are of any use to you and therefore the time and effort they require does not give you a great return on investment.

These groups do not mean that you can or should not participate in other referral groups! If those groups work for you, have the right sorts of people and can give you a return for attending then brilliant, attend them also.

Your own groups turn you into the hub; keep you front of mind of your network and opens up new opportunities.

The Super Group

The super group is your referral group and is made up of 8-10 individuals that all have the same sort of clientele but don't compete with one another. This group should come together at the same day and time each month. The purpose of the group is to pass referrals, create new exposure and open new doors up for the other members of the group.

The agenda for your super group goes as follows:
1. After week 1 you will start with accountability and each person can go through what they did and committed to.
2. Goal For The Month – each person goes around and states their goal for the month. If people can help with the goal then they will commit to doing so.
3. Connection For The Month – each person goes around and states the connection they would like for the month. Maybe it is an industry or a specific person.
4. Action Item For The Month- each person goes around and states 2 things they would like group members to do for them this month.
5. What I Can Do For Others – each person goes around and makes a commitment on what they will do for the other people.

There is a simple tool that the group can use to track and keep a record of their meeting. You can find it at www.trello.com

The Profitability Partner
Your profitability partner is a strong individual relationship. This partnership is the top level of your referral system and you will speak with one another every week. This can be a phone call and should not take any more than 15 minutes to complete following the agenda below:
1. After week 1 you will start with accountability and each person will go through what they did and committed to.
2. Goal For The Week – each person states their goal for the week. If you can help with the goal then commit to doing so.
3. Connection For The Week – each person states the connection they would like for the week. Maybe it is an industry or a specific person.
4. Action Item For The Week- each person states the 3 things they would like the other person to do for them this week.
5. What I Can Do For Others – each person states their commitment on what they will do for the other person

The Successful Referral Master Has Strong Teams

The successful referral master gets their teams up and running as quickly as possible. They have a Super Group and 4-6 Profitability Partners all set up. This is the maximum a person can handle successfully (giving true quality time and effort to each partner).

The successful referral master understands that through collaboration and sharing of networks, more can be achieved and in a much faster time frame than trying to do it all themselves.

Don't... Be in a rush and get the wrong people into your groups. Follow your criteria and make sure that they have the right mindset and values to help other people.

Do what I do… The more HUBS you can create and be a part of, the more people you have helping you through their networks. I have created:
- A super group that we have turned into a weekly meeting rather than monthly
- 4 profitability partners that I strategically plan with weekly
- A networking event that I can invite my community to and bring new people in to meet others in my network
- A LinkedIn group to help others meet one another

Action Steps To Take

1. Find 1 or 2 Profitability Partners to begin your referral teams, this is the quickest and easiest to set up. So start here.
2. Start interviewing people about being part of your Super Group. When you have 6 you can begin and add the others as you go.
3. Continue to add the next few Profitability Partners

4. See how you add an online or offline "HUB" to bring more of your community together.

How I Can Help You Immediately

We have a high level group that we call "The Partnership Platinum Club" and it brings invited only people to come together for one full day and create new opportunities with one another through Joint Ventures and Cross Promotions.

If this sounds like something you could me interested please pop onto this link and take a look –
www.thepartnershipclub.com.au/guestpass

Chapter 7: Turning Your Business Into A Hub and Community

Many businesses are so stuck doing the day-to-day work, creating the next sale, planning for the next 30 days, 60 days or a year that they lose sight of the 'real' big picture. This is a classic symptom of the scarcity mindset, by the way – allowing the daily challenges to dilute the passion of their vision!

I say that many business owners lose sight of the 'real' big picture because for any business to go to the top they need a community that is made up of prospects, past clients, current clients, partners, suppliers and your network. This is "thinking big" – beyond "what is" and thinking of "what can be." To achieve this, you will see both yourself and your business go to a whole new level. Many businesses only concentrate on their current clients (which admittedly can take a lot of energy and resources) but in so doing, they miss out on the other 80% of opportunities.

Your business should have a plan to create walking billboards, raving fans and people constantly speaking about you and what you do, whether you are there or not. In other words, have a tribe of people passionate about what you do, so that they promote you and spread the message for you!

Your business needs to make it easy and desirable for people to be a part of your community, whether it's on social media, through webinars, podcasts, videos or at live events. The more you connect with your community, *the more you help them* and the more you add value for them, the more they will want to promote you.

Build strong relationships with everyone in your community and then let your community know what you would like them to do for you. It's a win-win!

The Successful Referral Master Has a Strong and Passionate Community

The successful referral master is always looking at how to build strong hubs and communities, how to build engagement into everything they do and build and maintain strong relationships with their people. Then they work out how to create opportunities with the people in their community.

It is a simple equation: Network + Relationship = Referral Opportunities. By building Hubs and Communities you are instantly doing both network and relationship together.

The successful referral master knows that the more walking billboards they have, the more opportunities will be created for them.

Don't... just build databases to email weekly without any real relationship. The saying use to be "the money is in the list," however in today's society "the money is in the relationship with the list." Anyone can send out 100,000 emails, but the person who sends out 100,000 emails and gets 50,000+ opened is the winner.

Do what I do... I take growing our community and the relationship with each person within our community very seriously. I ensure that our team understands the importance and they are well trained on this aspect of the business. We actually have business 'KPI's' that measure the success of what we are doing.

There are two focuses:
1. Growing the community everyday with new people
2. Building and keeping relationships with those people in the community

We build the community by creating partnerships with other people who have the same sort of clientele as we do; this is the fastest way to get a lot of new people finding out about us in one go.

We then provide them with value through videos, groups, events, connections, templates, webinars, checklists and other opportunities that will add value to them.

We want to make a touch to each person within our community at least every 90 days *to see what they are up to, not to sell to them.*

Action Steps To Take

1. Start communicating with everyone in your current network and see what they are up to and doing
2. Encourage them to join your community on social media
3. Create a LinkedIn group or Facebook group for your community to come together online
4. Create a live event that brings your community together – something like a meetup; you can use www.meetup.com to organise this
5. Create an engagement plan so that you have consistent touch points and value adding opportunities for your community

How I Can Help You Immediately

Do you have a business community and would like to collaborate? We are always looking for good people with business communities to do things with. Email us at support@referralmarketingguru.com.au and let us know your thoughts?

Case Study #4: A Local Business Takes 45 Days To Be Full

Local businesses often don't believe that they have the support or people around them to build partnerships and create opportunities with the local community. This is a myth and a local business can dominate their niche in their area very easily.

This local business was in a regional area, there were less than 10,000 in its population and there were another 20 similar businesses that did exactly the same thing. So the market was certainly full.

This business provided personal training services to the public; they didn't have a defined target group and ran a number of both individual sessions and group sessions throughout the morning and evening.

They had always relied upon handing out fliers, going to a few networking events and having their current clients bring along friends.

They were operating at 40% of capacity so there was plenty of room to grow, so this is what we suggested that they do.

First we got them to create a similar DL Flier that could be used as a gift card to get 50% off. So many people do 7 days, free trial, etc. If you want to catch the fish you need a 'BIG' offer that will bring them in.

They then went around to all the cafes, restaurants and local shops to find the businesses and shared their vision and plan to see if they would like to use this gift card to hand out to their customers.

48 local businesses loved the idea and this meant that they were getting exposure all around town. The real key was

keeping the relationships with these other businesses and making sure that their clients also went in and used them.

What they had created was their own little hub of partnerships and loyalty.

Next they made contact with a dozen other health professionals to see who wanted to be part of their referrals super team. Within 30 days there were a group of 8 local health businesses meeting every fortnight to strategies on getting new business for one another.

With those plans now in place it only took 45 days for the business to be at 100% capacity and they were looking at bringing on more team members.

This shows again the power of collaboration and working with other people rather than trying to do it all yourself.

Chapter 8: Your Success Will Be Determined By Your Communication

You now have the wheels in motion, momentum is building and you have your teams underway. To be honest, there is ONLY ONE THING that will let you down: *your communication with your teams, hubs and communities.*

Effective communication results in more business every time. You may have great products and services, yet if you do not know how to communicate the benefits to your partners, how do you expect them to promote or pass referrals to you?

Communication is first about understanding your own preferred style (how you like to be communicated to) and then understanding your Partners' styles and their preferred method.

Some people just want to know the bullet points, brief and to the point. Some want the excitement, energy and fun; others want the details, all the steps and process on how best to refer. Finally, others may want to really understand the benefits on all areas of the business, the story behind how you got there and WHY you are doing what you are doing.

You might know some of the above styles. The easiest and efficient way to identify your own style and your Partner's is to complete the personality profile test, DISC. DISC is an easy 5min online test that will provide a solution to maximise your communication and business with your Partners.

The Successful Referral Master is a Master Communicator!

The successful referral master is constantly learning how best to communicate more effectively with their Partners to make it as easy and efficient for them to refer business. The successful referral master understands their Partner's preferred style of communication. This includes how to write emails, talk on the phone, in meetings, your referral manual, and how best to pass on referrals.

Don't... Ignore this important chapter. If you are not getting referrals from your Partners, then look at how you are communicating with them. Don't think that you shouldn't change or adapt your communication style as this can cause mis-understandings, confusion and lack of trust.

Do what I do... Take the time to understand your own communication style. Then enroll your Partners to do the same. This will further build trust and your referral partner relationship. Remember, we like referring business to those we know and trust. This is a great way to enhance this relationship.

Action Steps To Take

First understand yourself; then you will find it easier to understand others.
1. Complete your own DISC profile
2. Go through the results and see where your communication style has worked or hasn't worked in the past
3. Get your Partners to complete the DISC profile
4. Swap your Profiles and read through them together so that you start to understand what is important to each other
5. Adapt your style based on the results from the profile
6. Have some fun with adapting your newfound communication styles with your Partners, Team and Clients/Customers.

How I Can Help You Immediately

Seeing that you have committed in reading this book, then I would like to commend you for that. To make it even easier to

complete your DISC profile, simply go to
https://goalstribe.com/product/behaviour-style-profile-standard-report/

Here you will find the DISC profile with a 25% discount when you use the coupon code "the networker".

For more information on how best further understand the power of DISC and Communication with your Referral Partnership and your business, simply go to
www.goalstribe.com

Chapter 9: Putting Your System All Together

This chapter is a little different, as we have broken down every aspect of your referral marketing system. It is now time to put it into a simple to follow blueprint.

There are 4 main activities I concentrate on EVERY Day that gets me to be;
1. Front of mind with my network
2. Communicating with my network
3. Adding value to my network
4. Creating new opportunities with my network

These 4 activities will ensure that you get new referrals and opportunities each day.

First I find 25 people to stay front of mind of with our 'Community Engagement Plan.' This plan allows us to touch base with people in our network. We do this through making phone calls, sending a personal email, sending a personal social media message or using hand written cards.

All of these are personal touch points and in today's society that STANDS OUT from what everyone else is doing. You must ask yourself how do you have personal touch points and be remembered by your network.

Next we have a "Social Media Engagement Plan" that allows us to be shared, liked and commented on by our social media network. The importance of this is that you then get into new networks and new people whom you don't even know can find you. The social media engagement plan allows you to be seen by new possible partners, this means creating new collaboration opportunities every day.

With our plan we post our blogs, articles, podcasts and videos across all the major social media platforms every day. You can't just do this for a few weeks and then stop. Use tools like hootsuite to schedule posts for months in advance.

Thirdly we have a "Partner Engagement Plan," this plan is about the opportunities we are creating between us and our partners including webinars, podcast interviews, live events, recording videos or articles. All these items are to add value to the new network so that any interested people will come over and join our community.

The partner plans are very important as they allow you to get into new networks and have other people fill your sales funnel for you. The more partners you have, the better you communicate with them, the better your relationship with them, the more opportunities you will create.

Finally we are always looking for more partners to build relationships with. We look in social media platforms, online, networking events, and through communicating with our network – and this is an essential daily activity!

Either you have to find new qualified leads each day or you can leverage into other people's networks. Therefore the more partners, the more networks and the more opportunities.

How I Can Help You Immediately

After 6+ years of working it out we have created various step-by-step systems for referral marketing, networking, community engagement and creating joint venture opportunities.

You now can also have the exact same referral systems that we use each day in our business. The Partnership VIP Club gives you all these systems PLUS a new network from around the world to create new partnerships with. To find out more visit – www.referralmarketingguru.com.au/partnershipvipclub

Chapter 10: In Conclusion

In today's society there is so much noise, so many marketing messages and the consumer is being pulled in every direction. So who do they listen to? What do they hear? How do you get them to listen to *you*?

People will always listen to those that they 'know', 'like' and 'trust.'

When you can piggyback on someone else's credibility then you already have an advantage compared to those people who have no relationship.

That is the power of creating strategic partnerships and leveraging into other people's networks through their credibility.

Word of mouth marketing will always be the number #1 way to grow your business but as you have just seen, you need to create a referral plan and system, and not just leave it up to luck.

You have a financial plan, a business plan, an overall marketing plan, you set goals and performance indicators so why wouldn't you create a partnership plan to maximise the opportunities that are around you.

I certainly hope you have found this book to be valuable and encourage you to take action. Those that are successful are those that are doers!

Visit each chapter again, use the various links, be around the right people and begin your partnership plan right now.

www.ingramcontent.com/pod-product-compliance
Lightning Source LLC
Chambersburg PA
CBHW070923180526
45168CB00005B/2122